LOOK & FIND
ANIMALS

CREATED BY EUGENIYA POPOVA AND LILU RAMI

ILLUSTRATED BY MARGARITA KUKHTINA

CLEVER
Publishing

CATS

FIND EIGHT
BALLS OF
YARN.

COUNT
THE YELLOW
CATS.

HOW MANY
KITTENS DO
YOU SEE?

FIND ALL
THE MICE!

WHICH CAT IS
THE FLUFFIEST?

FIND SEVEN
STRIPED CATS.

DOGS

FIND THE PINK POODLES!

WHERE IS THE SMALLEST DOG?

RACCOONS

PANDAS

FIND ALL
THE SLEEPING
PANDAS.

ONE BABY PENGUIN
IS HIDING AMONG
THE PANDAS. CAN
YOU FIND HIM?

FIND THE
PANDA WEARING
A PARTY HAT!

ELEPHANTS

FIND ALL
THE ELEPHANTS
SPLASHING
IN THE WATER.

WHICH
ELEPHANT
IS GREETING
A MOUSE?

FIND
THE HIPPO!

CROCODILES

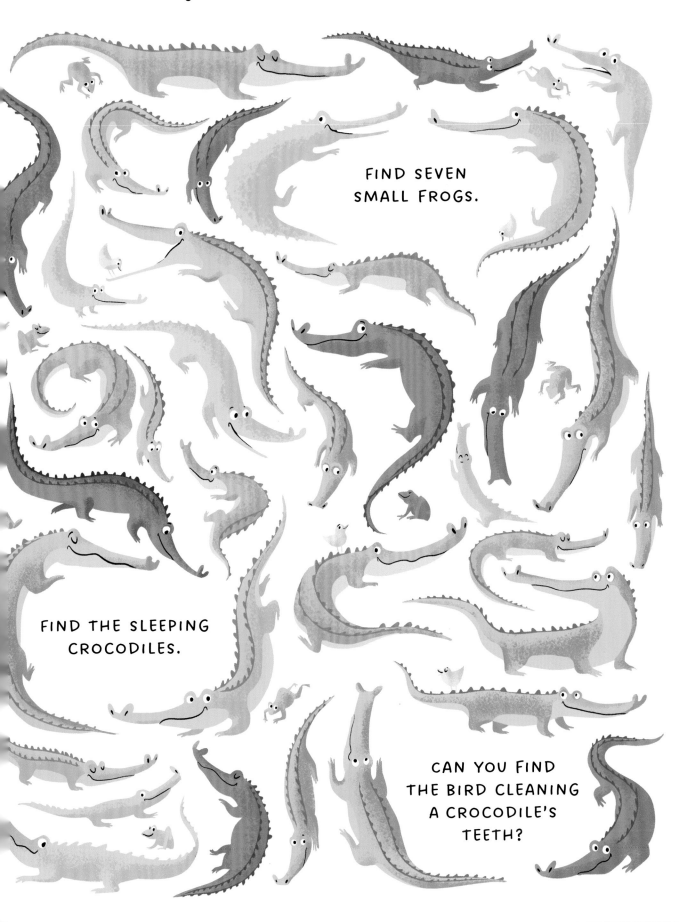

FIND SEVEN SMALL FROGS.

FIND THE SLEEPING CROCODILES.

CAN YOU FIND THE BIRD CLEANING A CROCODILE'S TEETH?

WOLVES

FIND THE HOWLING WOLVES.

WHERE IS THE BUNNY HIDING?

FIND THREE WOLF CUBS.

FOXES

COUNT THE SMALL FOXES.

FIND THE FOX WITH THE LARGEST TAIL.

HELP FIND THE LITTLE MOUSE.

OWLS

MICE

BUTTERFLIES

FIND ALL THE
DRAGONFLIES.

FIND
THE YELLOW
BUTTERFLIES.

COUNT
ALL THE PINK
BUTTERFLIES.

PARROTS

FIND
THE PIRATE
PARROT.

FIND TWO
PIGEONS AND
TWO TOUCANS.

WHERE ARE
THE LOVEBIRDS?

BUNNIES

FIND THE BUNNY HOLDING A PAINTBRUSH.

FIND THE BUNNY WITH THE LONGEST EARS.

HOW MANY BUNNIES ARE TAKING A NAP?

HEDGEHOGS

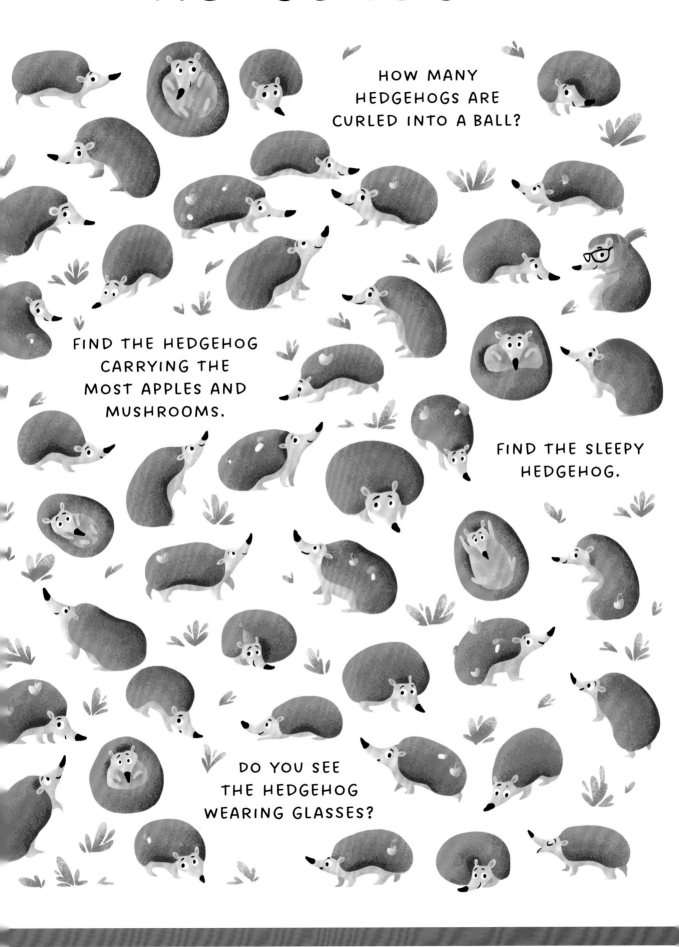

HOW MANY HEDGEHOGS ARE CURLED INTO A BALL?

FIND THE HEDGEHOG CARRYING THE MOST APPLES AND MUSHROOMS.

FIND THE SLEEPY HEDGEHOG.

DO YOU SEE THE HEDGEHOG WEARING GLASSES?

BEARS

FIND THE BEAR WITH THE BIGGEST SMILE.

HOW MANY SNOWMEN CAN YOU FIND?

WHICH BEAR HAS CAUGHT A DELICIOUS FISH?

HOW MANY BEARS ARE WEARING HATS?

PENGUINS

CAN YOU FIND THE BABY PENGUIN HATCHING FROM AN EGG?

HOW MANY PENGUINS ARE WEARING TIES?

FIND THE SNOWMAN!

HORSES

FIND THE LITTLEST HORSES.

FIND THREE HORSES WITH GRAY SPOTS.

HOW MANY HORSES ARE WEARING SADDLES?